The Statue of Liberty: The History and L Statue

By Charles River

A picture of Wilbur Wright flying near the Statue of Liberty in 1909

About Charles River Editors

Charles River Editors provides superior editing and original writing services across the digital publishing industry, with the expertise to create digital content for publishers across a vast range of subject matter. In addition to providing original digital content for third party publishers, we also republish civilization's greatest literary works, bringing them to new generations of readers via ebooks.

Sign up here to receive updates about free books as we publish them, and visit Our Kindle Author Page to browse today's free promotions and our most recently published Kindle titles.

Introduction

The Statue of Liberty

"[A] masterpiece of the human spirit [that] endures as a highly potent symbol—inspiring contemplation, debate and protest—of ideals such as liberty, peace, human rights, abolition of slavery, democracy and opportunity." - The UNESCO "Statement of Significance" describing the Statue of Liberty

Among America's countless monuments and landmarks, none embody the principles of the nation quite like Lady Liberty, the colossal statue that stands on Liberty Island in New York Harbor. A gift from the French that was built and transported in the late 19th century, the Statue of Liberty has been a symbol of the United States' guaranty of individual freedom, and its location took on added meaning as it welcomed millions of immigrants sailing across the Atlantic to nearby Ellis Island. As one incoming Greek immigrant remembered, "I saw the Statue of Liberty. And I said to myself, 'Lady, you're such a beautiful! [sic] You opened your arms and you get all the foreigners here. Give me a chance to prove that I am worth it, to do something, to be someone in America.' And always that statue was on my mind."

People around the world are instantly familiar with the statue today, whether from seeing pictures or depictions of it or actually visiting it and going inside, but the story of its construction is just as fascinating. Conceived as a monument that would commemorate the crucial alliance between America and France, the statue was a massive undertaking, from fundraising to the construction of the sculpture and a pedestal. The project took several years and a precarious transport of the statue's pieces across the Atlantic to New York, where it was officially dedicated in 1886 and celebrated with a ticker tape parade. Even before that, the statue was so famous on both sides of the Atlantic that the head and torch had been displayed at various exhibits prior to the completion of the statue.

Ironically, given the widespread fame of the Statue of Liberty, its history was turbulent and controversial. While those who conceived of the statue had a difficult time securing the funding, there were arguments over where the statue should go, and how everything from the pedestal to the statue itself should be built. In hindsight, it seems like a foregone conclusion that one of America's most famous monuments would be completed, but it would actually take almost 15 years for the Statue of Liberty to be designed, constructed, and completed, and the lion's share of the credit would go not to Americans but to dedicated French artists and engineers who pushed on with the work against major obstacles and heavy odds.

The Statue of Liberty: The History and Legacy of America's Most Famous Statue chronicles the design and construction of Lady Liberty. Along with pictures of important people, places, and events, you will learn about the Statue of Liberty like never before, in no time at all.

The Statue of Liberty: The History and Legacy of America's Most Famous Statue

About Charles River Editors

Introduction

Chapter 1: A Little Recital

"The account which I have been asked to prepare of the work of the French-American Union, of its history and its accomplishment, is a somewhat delicate thing for me to do, because of the difficulty of treating properly a subject in which I am obliged often to speak of myself. Apart from this consideration, however, I willingly accept the task of preparing this account, because it allows me to rectify many errors and to give correct information to those interested in this question. … The origin of the work of the French-American Union is of so modest a character that it would be very difficult to search it out if I did not recount it myself. That makes necessary a little recital of some circumstances in my own life." - Frédéric Auguste Bartholdi

The United States of America is a unique country in many ways, not the least of which is that it is built on the dreams of others. Whether they were seeking gold or religious freedom or a chance to avoid prison, the nation was built by people who came to the country to pursue their dreams, and throughout the 19th century, immigrants poured in from around the world seeking a better life for their families. Thus, it is fitting that the foremost symbol of the country, the Statue of Liberty, was born out of the dreams of others from outside the nation.

Ironically, at the time that the very idea of such a monument came about, the United States was in the midst of the Civil War. In 1863, Édouard René Lefèbvre de Laboulaye, a law professor in France, lectured his students, "Why is it that this friendship [between France and America] has eroded? Why is it that the face of America is not so dear to us as it was in those days [of the Marquis de Lafayette and George Washington]? It is due to slavery; we had always hoped that something would be done to put an end to an institution which was regarded by the founders of the Constitution as fraught with peril to the country; but instead of this, the partisans of slavery, having obtained the ascendant, have continually been engaged in efforts to perpetuate it and extend its limits, so that we have ceased to feel the same interest in Americans."

Édouard René Lefèbvre de Laboulaye

When the Civil War ended and slavery was abolished by the 13th Amendment, Laboulaye was ecstatic, he and told some friends at a dinner party in Versailles, "If a monument should rise in the United States, as a memorial to their independence, I should think it only natural if it were built by united effort—a common work of both our nations." According to a brochure put out by the National Park Service, "With the abolition of slavery and the Union's victory in the Civil War in 1865, Laboulaye's wishes of freedom and democracy were turning into a reality in the United States. In order to honor these achievements, Laboulaye proposed that a gift be built for the United States on behalf of France. Laboulaye hoped that by calling attention to the recent achievements of the United States, the French people would be inspired to call for their own democracy in the face of a repressive monarchy."

While Laboulaye's remarks might not have qualified as a commission for the project, they certainly inspired one of his guests, the famous French sculptor Frédéric Auguste Bartholdi. Then 30 years old, Bartholdi always had the soul of an artist; when he was just two years old, his mother wrote, "His body is very strong and robust, and his eyes and complexion and hair are all black. He is a very good child, very talkative. His faculties are fairly developed for his age, but his character needs to be guided a little differently from that of the older child, it will be a little more difficult. This child seems to me to carry with him the seed of a man with a strong and resolved character. Sometimes, at this age, one would call that character trait stubbornness, so it will be a matter of shaping that character without crushing it."

In writing about that dinner party decades later, Bartholdi remembered, "One evening, twenty years ago, I had been dining at the home of my most regretted and illustrious friend, M. Laboulaye, and his guests were smoking in the conservatory of his charming retreat, Glavigny, near Versailles, it was a gathering of men eminent in politics and letters. The talk fell upon international relations…M. Laboulaye observed…that in the United States they hold up to honor the remembrance of the common glories, they love Lafayette and his volunteers as they revere the American heroes. In the public mind this remembrance is much clearer than that of the political action of the French Government…every one recalls the names and the deeds of the French soldiers. There, said M. Laboulaye, is the basis of the sentiments which are felt in the United States toward the French, an indestructible basis, a sentiment honorable to the Americans as to us, and if a monument were to be built in America as a memorial to their independence, I should think it very natural if it were built by united effort, if it were a common work of both nations."

While he may have been stubborn, Bartholdi was no fool, and he knew only too well that in the 1860s, France was no great friend of the United States. Thus, he and Laboulaye kept their discussions quiet while he continued to work on other projects. He later recalled, "At this period I was expecting to execute a statue of Egypt for the Suez Lighthouse. I even laid before Ismail Pacha a project. It was this that made an evilly disposed newspaper say, and others repeat, that I had executed a colossal statue for Egypt, which had not been used."

In April 1869, he had a chance to impress the French emperor, Napoleon III, with his plans for a lighthouse to be built in Egypt. He wrote to his mother, "I am going to devote myself entirely to my Egypt business; it has the advantage of frankly showing its impossible side; but at least . . . I am seizing all means of possible support. I have excellent ones but with this, there is an aspect of the lottery and a play of luck is needed. I will do all that I can to seize the occasion…and if I fail, it is because there will not be a ghost of a chance. I showed my project to the Emperor and Empress. It seemed that all the world was enchanted, but they limited themselves to making wishes for my success…As little as this is, it permits me to say that there are [such] wishes without having to lie. I will equally have the support of Mr. Nieuwerkerke, [the head of the Louvre and director of the national museums]. By the end of the week, I will have collected all [the support] that I can get. After that, I will seize the bull by the horns."

As it turned out, the Franco-Prussian War broke out before Bartholdi had a chance to get his Egyptian project off the ground, so he instead spent much of the next two years serving as a major in the French militia. By the end of the war, France had lost his homeland, Alsace, and Napoleon III's monarchy had been abolished, so Bartholdi figured the time was right to get out of France for a while. He later wrote, "After a short stay in Switzerland, I resolved to take a journey in order to withdraw myself from all the painful impressions of the year through which I had just passed, and the idea came to me of going to visit America."

According to Bartholdi, when he mentioned his plans to de Laboulaye, de Laboulaye encouraged him to go and told him, "Go to see that country. You will study it, you will bring back to us your impressions. Propose to our friends over there to make with us a monument, a common work, in remembrance of the ancient friendship of France and the United States. We will take up a subscription in France. If you find a happy idea, a plan that will excite public enthusiasm, we are convinced that it will be successful on both continents, and we will do a work that will have a far-reaching moral effect"

Chapter 2: A Sympathetic Curiosity

"These very men were too much Americans and citizens of the great free people to feel hatred toward France or to rejoice over the misfortunes of the nation which helped to create their new country, whose prosperity they enjoy to-day. All those comments, those varied opinions, excited my lively interest. I had always felt a sympathetic curiosity concerning America, and a lively desire to know the country." - Frédéric Auguste Bartholdi

Bartholdi took a ship across the Atlantic in June 1871 to look for a site for his next great project, and during the crossing, he read Victor Hugo's *Chastisements* and fell in love with "Stella," a poem written about the importance of freedom from oppressive governments. The poem ends with the words:

> "I am coming. Arise, virtue, courage, faith!
> Thinkers, wits, climb to the tower, sentinels!
> Eyelids open, light up eyes,
> Earth, move the furrow, live, awake noise,
> Get up, you who are sleeping! Because the one who follows me,
> The one who sends me ahead first,
> It is the angel Freedom, it is the giant Light!"

When he first arrived in America and sailed into New York Harbor, the entrance point to lower Manhattan, Bartholdi was struck by the size and location of Bedloe's Island, which arriving and departing ships sailed past. He described his thoughts at the time: "In the course of the voyage I formed some conceptions of a plan of a monument, but I can say that at the view of the harbor of New York the definite plan was first clear to my eyes. The picture that is presented to the view when one arrives at New York is marvelous; when, after some days of voyaging, in the pearly radiance of a beautiful morning is revealed the magnificent spectacle of those immense cities, of those rivers extending as far as the eye can reach, festooned with masts and flags; when one awakes, so to speak, in the midst of that interior sea covered with vessels, some giants in size, some dwarfs, which swarm about, puffing, whistling, swinging the great arms of their uncovered walking-beams, moving to and fro like a crowd upon a public place. It is thrilling. It is, indeed, the New World, which appears in its majestic expanse, with the ardor of its glowing life."

D. Ramey Logan's picture of Liberty Island

At the time, however, the future Liberty Island was necessarily love at first sight for Bartholdi, who actually spent much of his trip looking at different potential locations for his colossal vision. He jotted down in his diary, "I hurry out to get a first glimpse of the city and to study sites for my project—the Battery, Central Park, the islands in the harbor." Ironically, Bartholdi confided in a letter to his mother, "Each site presents some difficulty, but the greatest difficulty, I believe, will be the American character which is hardly open to things of the imagination…I believe that the realization of my project will be a matter of luck. I do not intend to attach myself to the project absolutely if its realization is too difficult."

Before long, he was back near Bedloe's Island, and eventually, he wrote, "Went to Staten Island by ferry-boat to study the open harbor. The little island seems to me the best site."

Once he had determined a site for his statue, Bartholdi next began to try to get to know the people for whom he would be creating it, but ironically, actually meeting individual Americans challenged his somewhat romantic views of the country and its liberty: "I greatly admire the institutions of the country, the patriotism, the sense of civic duty, the objectivity of the government…The lone individual can't escape. He has to live in this 'collectivity.' There are probably elements of great power in this nation, but the individual…lives like a drop in a rainstorm, unable to break away by clinging to a blade of grass."

Nonetheless, Bartholdi was certain that he had found the appropriate site to display his great work, so he moved on across the country: "It was necessary at the outset to Americanize myself a little, to become acquainted with the country, the persons and the things, to become familiar with all the difficulties in order to hit upon the means of triumphant success. I traveled from the East to the West, from the North to the South, and visited nearly all the great cities of the United States and a great number of little ones that have, perhaps, become very great ones which I should not now recognize. In short, I made an artistic journey through the cities, and through the wild regions as well, painting and designing, finding acquaintances everywhere; and I employed my time so well for five months that brought back a more general knowledge of the United States than many Americans possess."

Perhaps Bartholdi's best impression of the United States came from President Ulysses S. Grant, the war hero who was instrumental in leading the Union to victory. In July 1871, Bartholdi wrote, "I went to see President Grant, who received me very kindly. I found the sovereign of the United States installed in a most simple cottage…The garden is the size of a man's hand…few flowers and no trees whatever. … [He] listened with the greatest interest to the recital of my projects. He is a cold man, like most Americans. He has a very energetic physiognomy. He displays an affability that is reserved and simple, but at the same time genuine. There is no formality…One is received as by the simplest bourgeois. I met his children, and his gouty father-in-law seated by a spittoon…I show him my project. He likes it very much, thinks that securing the site will not be a difficult problem, that the project will be submitted to Congress. He offers me a cigar."

Having learned that Bedloe's Island was on federal land and thus a location that would be easy to use for a national monument, Bartholdi returned to New York to make a few sketches of the island: "Today, after having done some work on drawings for my projects, I went to the island which ought to be the site of the monument. It is admirably located for my purposes. Unfortunately, a fort is built upon it—so that there is a possible conflict with the Army. But I believe this difficulty will be resolved when a decision has been reached about the monument itself. That is the question. I believe this enterprise will take on very great proportions. If things turn out as I hope they will, this work of sculpture will become of very great moral importance."

Chapter 3: To Produce an Emotion

"I think that it may be timely to examine briefly the characteristics of colossal statuary, in view of the fact that the art has from time to time been the object of criticism. Many persons see in it only a striking production, and do not understand its peculiar laws, its difficulties, nor its artistic value. Colossal statuary does not consist simply in making an enormous statue. It ought to produce an emotion in the breast of the spectator, not because of its volume, but because its size is in keeping with the idea that it interprets, and with the place which it ought to occupy. It should be used only in dealing with a limited order of ideas." - Frédéric Auguste Bartholdi

Once back in France, Bartholdi presented what he had learned and the plans he had developed to Laboulaye and others, including historian Henri Martin. Martin recalled, "It was needful for us to discover a thought in harmony with the object to be attained. The artist presented it to us in a form that bore the stamp of genius. He had conceived the celebration of the anniversary of Independence, applying to it a sublime phrase which sums up the progress of modern times: 'Liberty Enlightening the World.' M. Bartholdi proposed to represent this great idea by a statue of colossal proportions which would surpass all that have ever existed since the most ancient times. We adopted this plan with enthusiasm. A committee was organized. Artists, public men, constituted bodies, general councils, municipal councils and chambers of commerce associated themselves in the enterprise, and the movement which had started from so modest an origin became a genuine national demonstration."

With their support, Bartholdi continued to work on his concept for what would become the Statue of Liberty. In considering how to represent the ideals of freedom and liberty that he wanted to express, he turned to two images frequently seen in Revolutionary America. The first of these was Columbia, of whom the 18th century poet Phyllis Wheatley wrote:

> "One century scarce perform'd its destined round,
>
> When Gallic powers Columbia's fury found;
>
> And so may you, whoever dares disgrace
>
> The land of freedom's heaven-defended race!
>
> Fix'd are the eyes of nations on the scales,
>
> For in their hopes Columbia's arm prevails."

Columbia was often depicted as wearing long robes of virginal white and leading the fledgling nation into future greatness.

An 1872 painting of Columbia leading pioneers across the American frontier

The other figure, a version of Libertas (the Roman goddess of freedom), was frequently seen on American coins during the middle of the 19th century and was also featured on the Statue of Freedom, which sat atop the Capitol. Libertas was equally popular in France as a symbol of its ever elusive republican goals.

An ancient Roman coin depicting Libertas

The Statue of Freedom

In writing about the design process, Bartholdi cited three considerations: "1st—In the character or the thought of the subject, which ought to be in harmony with the size of the work. 2d—In the suitableness of the site and the surroundings of the monument. 3d—In the understanding of the lines and the makeup which, in colossal works of art, are rendered necessary by the execution." As far as the first point was concerned, Bartholdi certainly believed that bigger was better: "Colossal statuary ought to be used only to symbolize figures of thoughts which are grand in themselves, and as far as possible, abstract The immensity of form should be filled with the immensity of thought, and the spectator, at the sight of the great proportions of the work, should be impressed, before all things else, with the greatness of the idea of which these ample forms are the envelope, without being obliged to have recourse to comparative measurements in order to feel himself moved."

Bartholdi wanted the statue to be standing and giving the impression of leadership, rather than sitting in such a way that suggested she demanded worship. With that in mind, he had to square that vision with the location on Bedloe's Island. He noted, "In regard to the choice of site, a study should be made of similar existing works in order clearly to perceive the most favorable conditions. The frame should lend itself to the subject It may be made upon improved architectural effects, by the flights of stairs which lead up to the statue and contribute to the monumental character, but above all a site favorable by its own nature should be sought. There is an instinct which ought to guide the artist, for he ought to turn Nature to account in such a way as to make her contribute to the aspect of the monument. The neighborhood of large masses should be avoided. The artist ought to choose his site in such a way that the lines of the ground and the coloring of the background will become his assistants in heightening the proper appearance of his work and the impression which it is to produce."

As committed as he was to the idea that his statue should be big, Bartholdi was just as concerned that it be uncluttered: "In regard to the execution of colossal works of art, I think, as I said above, that we find sure principles in the ancient works. The difficulty is to apply them to one's own age, that is to say, without servile imitation of ^ the forms imagined by other epochs and other races. I may cite for example the principle of great simplicity in the movement and in the exterior lines. The gesture ought to be made plain by the profile to all the senses. The details of the lines ought not to arrest the eye. The breaks in the lines should be bold, and such as are suggested by the general design. Beside the work should be as far as possible filled out, and should not present black spots or exaggerated recesses. The surfaces should be broad and simple, defined by a bold and clear design, accentuated in the important places. The enlargement of the details or their multiplicity is to be feared. By exaggerating the forms, in order to render them more clearly visible, or by enriching them with details, we would destroy the proportion of the work. Finally, the model, like the design, should have a summarized character, such as one would give to a rapid sketch. Only it is necessary that this character should be the product of volition and study, and that the artist, concentrating his knowledge, should find the form and the line in its greatest simplicity."

To start, Bartholdi drew and then molded his Liberty as an adult woman wearing a gown and cloak similar to that worn by Roman goddesses. Bartholdi was adamant that the statue be beautiful from every angle so that passengers on ships passing through New York Harbor could admire her, front and back, as they passed by. He also designed Liberty so that her hand held high a torch that lit the way to the future. In fact, the figure destined to grace New York harbor was primarily inspired by Bartholdi's earlier model for the Egyptian lighthouse: the large shape of a young slave girl holding a light up above her head. Some people later claimed that Lady Liberty also bore a striking resemblance to his mother, to whom he was very devoted.

At first, Bartholdi thought that Liberty might hold something like a broken chain in her left hand, but with slavery and the Civil War still fresh in everyone's minds, he came to see that idea as too divisive. Instead, the broken chain would go under her feet, in a way similar to statues of the Virgin Mary trampling the head of the serpent. This left her left hand free to hold a *tabula ansata*, a tablet symbolizing the role of law in American society. On the tablet, he planned to inscribe the date "JULY IV MDCCLXXVI." This was both a romantic and practical gesture, as it not only honored the date of the Declaration of Independence but also established a firm deadline to have the money raised and the statue completed by the time of the American centennial celebration.

Since the statue would be so large, Bartholdi knew that he could use the help of a good engineer, so he appealed to a friend, Eugène Viollet-le-Duc, for help. At the time, Viollet-le-Duc was best known for having created the gargoyles that adorned the top of Notre Dame, and he had also been one of Bartholdi's favorite instructors. Ultimately, Viollet-le-Duc was the one who determined that the best type of support for the statue would consist of a wooden frame covered first in plaster and then in copper plates, heated and hammered into place. Where necessary, the lead plates would be used to shape the copper further.

Eugène Viollet-le-Duc

The biggest question during the design phase was how to ensure such a tall statue would stand for generations, and Viollet-le-Duc came up with an idea that those given charge of Liberty's care always appreciated. The base below the waist would be filled with containers of sand, which would give the statue extra weight but also allow for easy repairs to the inside, since the containers could be emptied and moved when necessary. Viollet-le-Duc also tweaked Bartholdi's *stola* design so that it gave the statue a wider and thus more stable base to the structure, which by then was planned to be around 150 feet tall.

A picture of Bartholdi's design patent for the statue

Chapter 4: These Granite Beings

"To all those who have studied it, Egyptian art has been the object of profound admiration, not only in view of the masses, the millions of kilograms moved by the Egyptian people, but on account of its concrete and majestic character, in design and in form, of the works which we see. We are filled with profound emotion in presence of these colossal witnesses, centuries old, of a past that to us is almost infinite, at whose feet so many generations, so many million existences, so many human glories, have rolled in the dust. These granite beings, in their imperturbable majesty, seem to be still listening to the most remote antiquity. Their kindly and impassable glance seems to ignore the present and to be fixed upon an unlimited future. These impressions are not the result simply of a beautiful spectacle, nor of the poetry of historic remembrances. They result from the character of the form and the expression of the work in which the design itself expresses after a fashion infinity." - Frédéric Auguste Bartholdi

Bartholdi knew very early on that he had set out to do something special. As he later wrote, "Up to the present time no statue had ever been executed of the extraordinary proportions of the Statue of Liberty. In order to form an idea of this work, which was without precedent, it was necessary to give the greatest attention to the means of execution; it was necessary to foresee the elements of solidity and the exigencies of transportation to America; finally, it was necessary to seek to avoid heavy expenses, into which one is rapidly drawn in a work of this kind, according to the methods employed. The examination of the various difficulties led us to adopt the system of hammered copper, which, from an artistic point of view, offers elements of excellence when it is well treated, which allows of a large subdivision in the pieces, and renders the transportation easy."

Of course, as Bartholdi implied, the biggest obstacle to the project was securing the funds necessary to actually complete it. To get the fundraising process going, the French-American Union, a committee established to support the project, sent out a request for funds which began, "America is soon to- celebrate the hundredth anniversary of her independence. That date marks an epoch in the history of humanity: to the New World, it recalls her work, the foundation of the great Republic; to France, one of the most honorable pages in her history. In concert with our friends in the United States we think this is a befitting occasion for associating France and America in a common demonstration. In spite of the lapse of time, the United States love to recall our ancient fraternity in arms; always among them the name of France is held in honor. The great event which is to be celebrated on the Fourth of July, 1876, allows us to celebrate with our American brothers the old and strong friendship which for a long time has united the two peoples. The New World is preparing to give extraordinary splendor to that festival; friends of the United States have thought that the genius of France ought to display itself in a dazzling form."

The brochure then launched into a description of the statue it envisioned and offered an explanation as to why it was such an excellent idea: "A French artist has embodied that thought in a plan worthy of its object, and which is approved by all; he has come to an understanding with our friends in America, and has prepared all the means for executing the plan. It is proposed to erect, as a memorial of the glorious anniversary, an exceptional monument In the midst of the harbor of New York, upon an islet which belongs to the Union of the States, in front of Long Island, where was poured out the first blood for independence, a colossal statue would rear its head, outlined upon space, framed on the horizon by the great American cities of New York, Jersey City and Brooklyn. At the threshold of that vast continent, full of a new life, where arrive all the vessels of the world, the statue will rise upon the bosom of the waves. It will represent 'Liberty Enlightening the World.' At night a resplendent aureole upon its brow will throw its beams far upon the vast sea."

Having made their case, the authors of the appeal concluded "That monument will be executed in common by the two peoples, associated in this fraternal work as they were of old in founding independence. We will make a gift of the statue to our friends in America; they will unite with us in meeting the expenses of the execution and of the erection of the monument, which will serve as a pedestal. We will in this way declare by an imperishable memorial the friendship that the blood spilled by our fathers sealed of old between the two nations. Let us unite in the celebration of this festival of modem peoples. It is necessary for us to be numerous in order to give to that demonstration the brilliancy that it ought to have that it may be worthy of the past. Let us each bring his mite. The smallest subscriptions will be heartily welcomed. Let the number of signers testify to the sentiments of France."

The appeal was signed by Laboulaye, Martin and a number of others, including descendants of Alexander de Tocqueville and the Marquis de Lafayette.

In addition to passing out requests for support, Bartholdi and Laboulaye went out of their way to woo some of the wealthiest men and women in France by hosting exclusive dinner parties and giving lectures to civic groups. They also hoped to work with Victor Hugo to write an opera in honor of the project, but after Hugo refused, Charles Gounod, the author of *Faust*, became involved and composed a moving cantata called "Liberty Enlightening the World." Hoping to persuade Hugo to work with him, Gounod wrote to the famous author, "I will not dissimulate, Monsieur and illustrious Master that to achieve (or almost) this epic Ode or Hymn one must be a giant, or cling to the shoulder of a giant. I am not that giant: Do you want to be the shoulder of the giant for me?" Unfortunately, the cantata and his other fundraising efforts proved to be disappointing; during the first six months of active work, the committee was only able to raise about a quarter of the funds needed to complete the statue.

CHARLES GOUNOD.

Gounod

While one group was working in France to see the statue become a reality, another sub-committee was a hard at work in the United States raising funds to build the base on which Lady Liberty was to stand. Bartholdi visited the United States for a second time in 1877, during which he traveled to most of the major East Coast cities to encourage interest and support in the project. He was more successful in New York than he had been in Paris, as he was able to convince a number of prominent men, including a very young Theodore Roosevelt, to assist him in raising funds. The committee was also instrumental in persuading Congress to support the plan, primarily by providing the land on Bedloe's Island. In February 1877, Congress passed a "Joint Resolution, authorizing the President to designate and set apart a site for the colossal statue of 'Liberty Enlightening the World,' and to provide for the permanent maintenance and preservation thereof…" The resolution read:

"Whereas The President has communicated to Congress the information that citizens of the French Republic propose to commemorate the one hundredth anniversary of our independence by erecting, at their own cost, a colossal bronze statue of 'Liberty Enlightening the World,' upon a pedestal of suitable proportions, to be built by private subscription, upon one of the islands belonging to the United States in the harbor of New York; and Whereas It is proper to provide for the care and presentation of this grand monument of art, and of the abiding friendship of our ancient ally; therefore, be it Resolved, By the Senate and House of Representatives of the United States of America in Congress assembled, that the President of the United States be and he is hereby authorized and directed to accept the colossal statue of "Liberty Enlightening the World," when presented by citizens of the French Republic, and to designate and set apart for the erection thereof a suitable site upon either Governor's or Bedloe's Island, in the harbor of New York; and upon the completion thereof shall cause the same to be inaugurated with such ceremonies as will serve to testify the gratitude of our people for this expressive and felicitous memorial of the sympathy of the citizens of our sister Republic ; and he is hereby authorized to cause suitable regulations to be made for its future maintenance as a beacon, and for the permanent care and preservation thereof as a monument of art, and of the continued good will of the great nation which aided us in our struggle for freedom."

When Bartholdi returned to France, he commissioned opera backdrop designer Jean-Baptiste Lavastre to create a backdrop designed to help those in Paris, most of whom would never visit the United States, to see what he saw when he first landed in New York. The resulting 36 foot tall painting was a rousing success; according to one reporter, "By some incredible feat of trompe-l'oeil, you are all of a sudden looking out over the stern of an American steamboat on her way out of New York harbor. Very near you, on the bridge, are life-sized people, dressed Yankee-fashion, smoking and talking; a little farther away more people are clustered together on the bridge, and farther off yet the pilot stands at the helm. Over his head floats the ensign with its silver stars…But let us turn our eyes away from our ship to the spectacle which invites our attention. All around us, on the choppy waters, sailboats and steamboats of all kinds are moving, fast or slow, in all directions…The traffic is unbelievable…and now, from her island, rises the gigantic Statue of Liberty, illuminating the world with the rays of her electric beacon…All around is the beautiful harbor; beyond it, the huge city…with its endless streets and avenues, an ocean of houses as big as the Atlantic itself."

With that, donations for Lady Liberty began to pour in.

Chapter 5: Colossal Proportions

"To give at that time in America an idea of the work, the right hand of the statue was executed in its colossal proportions and sent to the Exposition at Philadelphia. … These circumstances, which awaken patriotic feelings, gave an opportunity for getting the American public earnestly interested in the grand project of their French friends. … I executed the head of the statue for the Paris Exposition of 1878. In the following year all the funds necessary for the execution of the statue were obtained. On July 7, 1880, the sending of the official notification to the American Committee of the progress of the work and of the date when the labors upon it would be completed, was celebrated by a fete given to General Noyes, the United States Minister at Paris. This notification was sent to the United States upon an illuminated parchment signed by the members of the Committee and all the Frenchmen who were present." - Frédéric Auguste Bartholdi

1876 picture of the torch-bearing arm on display in Philadelphia

Once some of the funding was in place, Bartholdi could begin working on the statue in earnest, and in addition to being a master artist, Bartholdi was also something of a fundraising genius. He made it his mission to use every phase of Lady Liberty's construction to stir up more interest and thus more funding. As he later pointed out, "The total height of the first model was 1.25 meters. This was the study model which was long sought and often recast. (It is the model which has been reproduced in terra-cotta, the number of the reproductions being limited to two hundred. Each model was numbered and registered, and a large number of them were sold in aid of the subscription under the name of the 'Model of the Committee.'"

A picture of a small model of Lady Liberty

After carefully studying and making notes on his first model, Bartholdi made another, larger, sample of the work that would give him a better sense of how the finished product would look. He wrote, "After this first study I made the statue which measures from the head to the feet 2.8 meters, and in its entirety 2.85 meters. This statue, executed with rigid precision, was reproduced four times as large by the ordinary processes. The model which was the result of this work measured about 11 meters in total height. Placed in a large space it could be taken in by the eye in its entirety, and the corrections to be made could still be noted. This statue was divided into a large number of sections destined to be reproduced separately at four times their size. After this last enlargement changes were no longer possible. Now the sculptor could only aim at very great precision, and at great care in the modeling of the surfaces, which were becoming enormous."

As Bartholdi mentioned, since the statue was going to be so large, Lady Liberty would obviously have to be built in pieces in France so that it could be transported by ship to America.

Always planning, Bartholdi decided to turn this problem into an advantage by building the statue a piece at a time and then displaying individual pieces in tour exhibits to stir up interest in and raise more money for the project.

His first step was to create the right hand, which held the iconic torch. Working in a workshop owned by Gaget, Gauthier & Co., a place he described as "an immense workshop, specially constructed for the work," he began construction. He later wrote that there "were to be seen four plane surfaces on which the work was carried on. They were encompassed with frames laid out in numbered divisions. Another similar frame, corresponding exactly to the one below, was fastened beneath the ceiling of the workshop. Lead wires and rulers hung all around the frames. On these frames, thus geometrically laid out, the sculptors executed, in wood and in plaster, enormous fragments of the statue. The sections of the model that they were to reproduce were arranged nearby under corresponding conditions, between frames of one-fourth the size. The sculptors executed the enlargement by measurements taken with the compass on the lead wires and the rulers."

Thus, it was hoped, different men working in different places off of identical models would be able to create pieces that could eventually be joined together in a harmonious whole. Of course, in order for this to happen, their processes had to be both precise and identical. Bartholdi explained the steps: "They first laid out the general form with wooden beams covered with lath work. The wood was then covered with a coating of plaster. They verified the large measurements already established, and then executed the reproduction point by point, and finished the modeling of the surfaces. Each nail head and point marked requires six measurements, three on the model and three for the enlargement without counting the verifying measurements. There were in each course about 300 large points and more than 1,200 secondary points, which represented for each course, the work of establishing about 9,000 measurements."

Once the base for each portion of the structure was completed, it was time to apply the iconic copper covering, laid in sheets about as thick as two stacked pennies. The copper itself had a story to tell, as it had come from a number of different mines and was donated by several different companies. The lion's share, nearly 130,000 of the 200,000 pounds of copper used, was given by Eugène Secrétan, while Japy Frères donated most of the rest. Bartholdi later described how the copper was applied: "When a course was finished the carpenters took its forms by means of boards cut in profile, according to the form of the plaster. They were applied on the spot, placed one opposite to another and crossed, thus forming pigeon-holes, larger or smaller. Thus they took a sort of impression. In these wooden molds or "gabarits," the hammers pressed the sheets of copper by pressure with levers, and by hammering with mallets. The pieces of copper were finished by beating them with little hammers and with rammers. The profile of the forms was again taken in detail with sheets of lead, pressed upon the model, again working the copper according to the profiles. The pieces of copper were furnished from point to point with iron braces, intended to give then rigidity. These braces were forged in the form of the copper when the contour of the latter was completely modeled. Thus furnished, the pieces were carried to the mounting in the court, to be brought together and fastened on the powerful truss work of iron beams which serves as support for the whole envelope of the statue. The core of this truss work is formed by a sort of pylon which has four points of attachment. Each of these points is sustained by three bolted braces, fifteen centimeters in diameter, which are made fast at a depth of eight meters in the masonry of the foundation to a frame of iron beams."

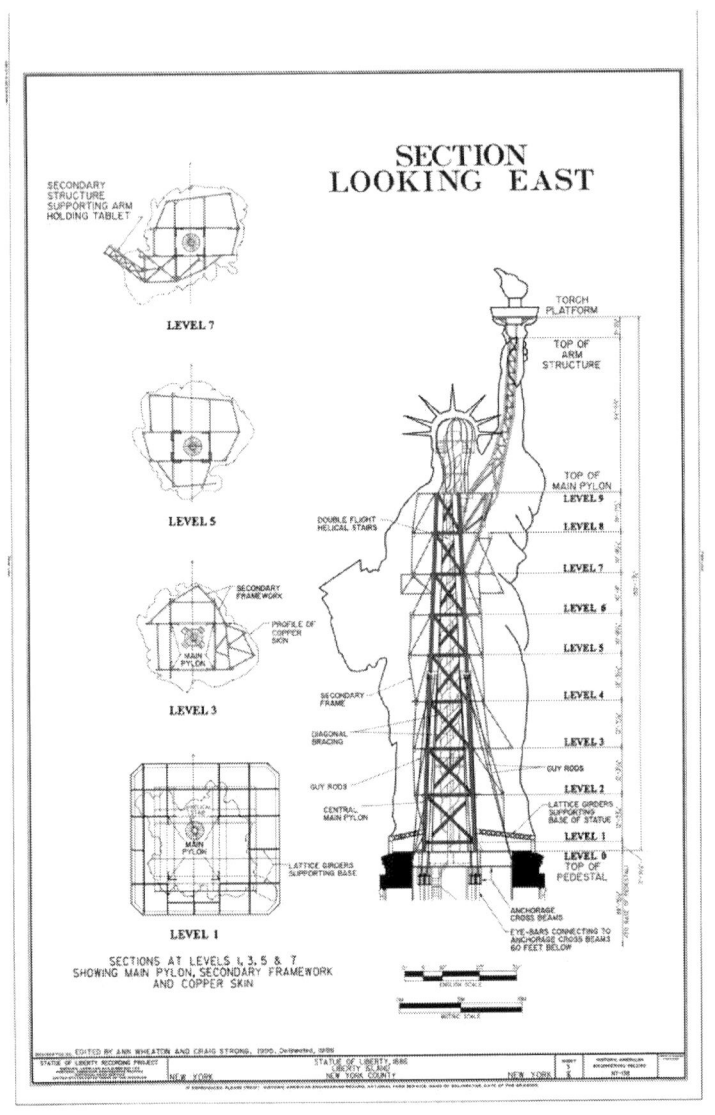

Picture of a blueprint of the statue

Chapter 6: Heavy Expenses

"Up to the present time no statue had ever been executed of the extraordinary proportions of the Statue of Liberty. In order to form an idea of this work, which was without precedent, it was necessary to give the greatest attention to the means of execution; it was necessary to foresee the elements of solidity and the exigencies of transportation to America; finally, it was necessary to seek to avoid heavy expenses, into which one is rapidly drawn in a work of this kind, according to the methods employed. The examination of the various difficulties led us to adopt the system of hammered copper, which, from an artistic point of view, offers elements of excellence when it is well treated, which allows of a large subdivision in the pieces, and renders the transportation easy." - Frédéric Auguste Bartholdi

In May 1876, Bartholdi returned to the United States again to promote his project. He had hoped to have the hand and torch finished by then so that it could be available for the Centennial celebrations, but since that didn't happen, he instead presented the people of America with a gigantic painting of the statue as he planned it to look upon its completion. This succeeded it stirring up interest, and when the hand finally arrived in August, it became a popular feature of the exhibition.

However, not everyone was thrilled with the idea of the colossal work. A *New York Times* editorial that appeared on September 29, 1876 complained, "It is true that at first the story that the Frenchmen intended to make us so large a present was received with some degree of incredulity, especially as the illustrated papers promptly published pictures of the statue with a lighted torch in its right hand and an enthusiastic public consisting of four men and three women standing in admiration at its base...Events have apparently justified the fears...A dismal report now reaches us from France that work upon the statue has been suspended in consequence of a lack of funds...From present appearances we have now all of the statue that we shall have unless we are willing to pay the cost of finishing it and it is more than doubtful if the American public is ready to undertake any such task. For the feeblest mathematician can easily calculate that if it costs 200,000 francs to make one arm of the proposed statue, it will cost a great many times that amount to finish it."

One thing the arm demonstrated was that Bartholdi was not just completing a statue but a structure that people would be able to visit and tour on the inside as well. Those visiting the exhibit in Philadelphia enjoyed being able to climb through the arm and up on to the balcony around the torch. From that height, as many as 40 people at a time could see the entire fairground. In order to keep interest up after the exhibition ended, Bartholdi had the arm moved to New York City, where it remained on display in Madison Square Park for years until it was finally sent back to France to be part of the completed statue.

Once back in France, Bartholdi moved on to the next major piece of the statue, and he spent weeks preparing her head to be exhibited in 1878's Universal Exposition in Paris. One reporter wrote, "Long before the head reached the Champ de Mars my curiosity as to this stupendous specimen of womanhood took me to the workshop in the Rue Chazelle, near the Parc Monceau, where it is being made." Once at the shop, he observed men "hammering for their lives on sheet copper to complete the toilet of her tresses for the show...I mounted the scaffolding with them and stood on the level of her awful eye some thirty inches from corner to corner to be engulfed in her gaze...Her lips, from dimple to dimple, were as long as my walking-stick, and fifteen people, I was told, might sit around the flame of her torch." Of the artist himself, the reporter wrote, "Bartholdi is an Alsacian as well as a Frenchman, still young for an artist of his reputation—I should not give him a day more than forty, sincere and winningly bold in manner, of middle height, dark, large-featured, and with a very penetrating glance. He gives you the impression of a man of power, and his works confirm it. He loves to model on a colossal scale perhaps because this most readily conduces to the simplicity and massiveness of effect which he seeks in art."

Pictures of the head on exhibit at the Paris World's Fair in 1878

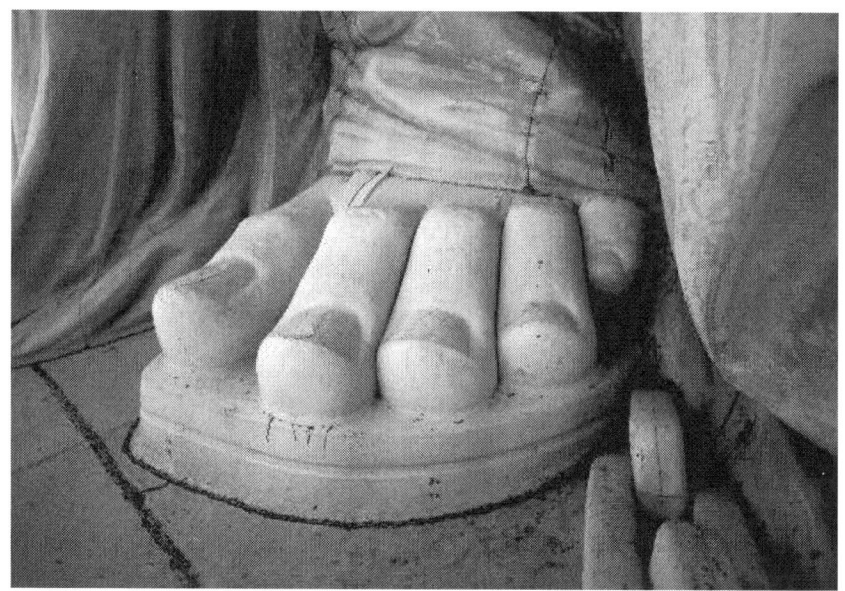

A picture of the statue's toes

In spite of his best efforts, the reporter did not get much of an interview out of Bartholdi, who preferred to spend his time complaining about the faults he saw in other men's work. Still, seeing the interest in the man's eyes, Bartholdi conceived of a new fundraising scheme and began selling tickets for the public to come and watch him and his men at work.

Picture of workers constructing the statue

By the beginning of 1880, he was well over halfway to full funding for the project, but Bartholdi suffered a great loss when Viollet-le-Duc died. That is how Gustave Eiffel came to be involved in the project.

Eiffel

When he first joined, Eiffel had three things on his mind. First, there was the matter of how to create a structure that would be strong enough to support both Lady Liberty and the many people who would likely visit her each year. He had built large bridges before and was all too aware of the kind of beating a tall, thin structure takes from the weather. No one wanted to take the chance that a great storm might knock Lady Liberty into the sea.

To protect against this, Eiffel created a steel skeleton, building it in his own factory outside of Paris. Bartholdi later wrote, "The whole truss-work was designed and executed by the eminent constructing engineer, M. Eiffel. This truss work serves as a support for the copper form of the statue. The copper plates, kept in shape by iron bands, are supported by iron braces, which are cramped on to the central core. They do not bear in the least upon the lower plates, and their weight is always independent of all that is above and below." What made Lady Liberty's construction so special was the way in which Eiffel designed her to have a type of "curtain wall" construction in which each panel would hang on the iron framework instead of standing on a base. This allowed the structure to be supported all over, instead of just at her base.

Eiffel's next concern was how the statue would react to the constant temperature changes in New York Harbor. Indeed, one reporter publicly warned him, "The heat of the sun would expand the metal and pull it out of shape, precisely as it does pull the Brooklyn Bridge [then under construction] out of shape every day." To help cope with the slight shifts caused by temperature change, Eiffel installed sheets of heavy asbestos between the copper skin and the plaster underneath. This also helped protect the interior skin from corrosion.

Finally, since the statue was composed primarily of copper over iron, Eiffel and others worried that the constant exposure of saltwater might create some sort of "gigantic battery of unknown potential." Fortunately, this never proved to be a problem.

True to his promise that visitors would be able to go inside the great statue, Bartholdi had two staircases built into the statue, allowing those with enough stamina to reach her head. However, the privilege of standing on the balcony around her torch would be reserved for only a chosen few, since that part of the structure could only be reached by a dangerous ladder that spanned the final 40 feet.

A picture of First Lady Nancy Reagan in 1986

With the changes Eiffel made, Bartholdi was able to make some changes of his own and complete the statue in one piece in Paris before shipping it to America. By 1882, Lady Liberty was complete from the waist down, and as part of a unique press event, Bartholdi treated a group of reporters to lunch inside his colossal creation. By 1884, the statue was completed in full and Bartholdi ceremoniously presented it to the United States Ambassador Levi Morton on July 4 of that year in a grand ceremony held in Paris. According to one record of the event, Ferdinand de Lesseps, the builder of the Suez Canal and president of the French-American Union, "thanked M. Bartholdi, who conceived and executed the immense statue, which may be characterized, said he, as the eighth wonder of the world. M. de Lesseps said that he was handing over to the United

States this great artistic monument, the gift of France, to which have contributed by their votes 180 cities, forty general councils, a large number of chambers of commerce and of societies, and over a hundred thousand subscribers. He thanked the modest co-workers, M. Bergerct, M. Baron, and particularly M. Simon, the brave assistant of M. Bartholdi. He dwelt upon the merit of the great industrial house, Gaget, Gauthier & Co., whose director, M. Gaget, was able so successfully to accomplish such extraordinary labors. He concluded by saying: 'This work, Mr. Minister, is the product of enthusiasm, of devotion of intelligence, and of the noblest sentiments which can animate man. It is great in its conception and in its realization^ It is colossal in its proportions, and we hope that it will grow still greater through its moral worth, thanks to the remembrances and the sentiments which it is to perpetuate. We commit it to your care, Mr. Minister, that it may remain forever the pledge of the bonds which should unite France and the great American nation.'"

Chapter 7: Born for this Place

"The colossal statues which have been executed up to the present time are far from the proportions of the Statue of Liberty. Yet we must not expect its appearance to be colossal when it is in its place. In the immense picture which will surround it, it will appear simply in harmony with the whole, and have the normal aspect of a statue in a public place. It should be thus, because its part is not to appear extraordinary in itself, but to connect itself intimately with an extraordinary whole. The statue was born for this place which inspired its conception. May God be pleased to bless my efforts and my work, and to crown it with the success, the duration and the moral influence which it ought to have. I shall be happy to have been able to consecrate the best years of my life to being the interpreter of the noble hearts whose dream has been the realization of the monument to the French-American Union." - Frédéric Auguste Bartholdi

In spite of all the hoopla, America was not yet ready to receive the gift because the pedestal was still incomplete. In fact, for a time it seemed that Lady Liberty would be all dressed up with nowhere to go. Less than a decade removed from the end of the Civil War, the country had experienced a major economic setback in 1873 and was still trying to recover. There were other regional and national projects vying for American's attention, including the Brooklyn Bridge, which had more practical purposes. On top of all that, the symbolism of Lady Liberty was not very appealing to a country more interested in erecting realistic statues to fallen heroes, and xenophobia reared its ugly head as some Americans wondered why they should contribute money to a base for a statue made in another country.

Despite the obstacles, Bartholdi would not give up, and he took every opportunity to answer criticisms and speak out on behalf of the project whenever he was in America. During one luncheon, he told those in attendance, "Her presence above the port of New York, will not allow Americans to forget that they have never had a friend more faithful and devoted than France. As each year misery grows in these widely separated lands, thousands of unfortunates want to both seek relief from their suffering and spread seeds of hatred against us, it is without doubt useful that there is something to recall that, a century ago, other men came to America, to take their part, not in its wealth, but in its dangers, to lend their strength to the oppressed and to help them conquer on the battlefields, this liberty which perhaps might have escaped them." One reporter who was at that luncheon wrote, "We have been glad to hear him explain the concept that gave birth to his giant statue, which more than one time we have heard accused of having the unique desire of astonishing the world."

A short time later, another story broke, with one paper announcing, "It was rumored to-day that the Bartholdi statue of 'Liberty,' which has been intended for Bedloe's Island, has been virtually offered to Boston." This stirred up strong feelings locally, but given the halting state of progress, another reporter chided readers that "in view of the facts no New Yorker will have the slightest right to complain if the statue goes to Boston [since]…absolutely nothing has been done."

All this talk was just the motivation New York needed to get busy. One newspaper asserted, "[Boston] proposes to take our neglected statue of Liberty and warm it over for her own use and glory. Boston has probably again overestimated her powers. This statue is dear to us, though we have never looked upon it, and no third rate town is going to step in and take it from us. Philadelphia tried to do that in 1876, and failed. Let Boston be warned…that she can't have our Liberty…that great light-house statue will be smashed into…fragments before it shall be stuck up in Boston Harbor. If we are to lose the statue it shall go to some worthier and more modest place—Painted Post, for instance, or Glover, Vt."

Among the efforts put forward to raise money for the pedestal was an art and manuscript auction, and one of the people approached for a donation was the poet Emma Lazarus, who the committee hoped would contribute an original piece inspired by the statue itself. She initially refused, insisting that she did not find such a piece inspirational, but after some volunteer work with Jewish refugees flooding into New York, she found a different inspiration from their stories. Thinking in terms of what such a piece might mean to them, she penned a sonnet called "The New Colossus."

"Not like the brazen giant of Greek fame,
With conquering limbs astride from land to land;
Here at our sea-washed, sunset gates shall stand
A mighty woman with a torch, whose flame
Is the imprisoned lightning, and her name
Mother of Exiles. From her beacon-hand
Glows world-wide welcome; her mild eyes command
The air-bridged harbor that twin cities frame.

'Keep, ancient lands, your storied pomp!' cries she
With silent lips. 'Give me your tired, your poor,

Your huddled masses yearning to breathe free,
The wretched refuse of your teeming shore.
Send these, the homeless, tempest-tost to me,
I lift my lamp beside the golden door!'"

Emma Lazarus

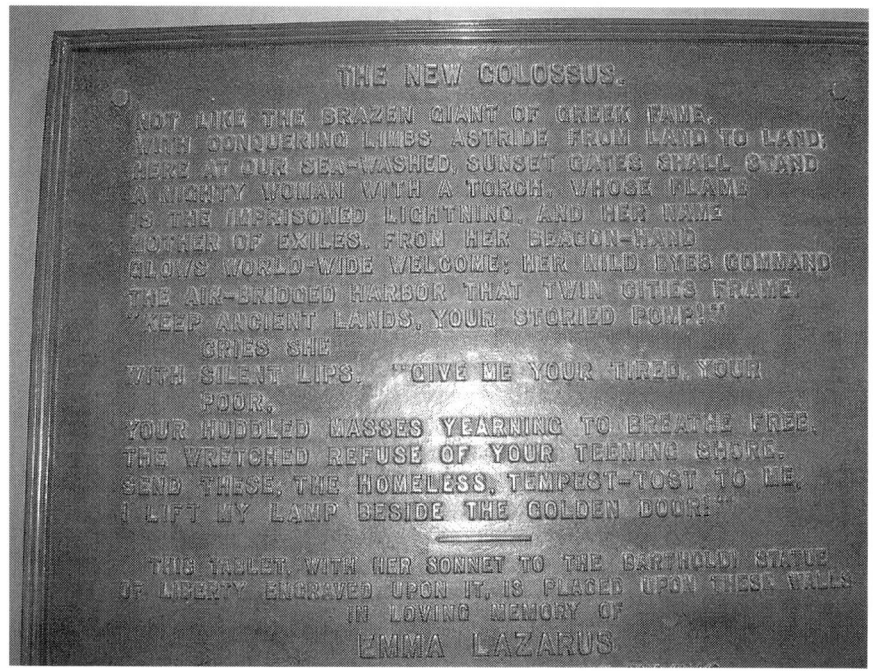

The plaque commemorating Emma Lazarus' poem

The last few lines, spoken from the perspective of Lady Liberty herself, were eventually engraved on the pedestal of the statue that Lazarus at first found uninspiring.

With money now coming in for the pedestal, the American contingent of the French-American Union got busy and began planning the precise location for the giant plinth. After some discussion, they determined that the best site for the statue would be inside the walls of Fort Wood, a former army base dating back to the early 1800s that was no longer in use. The artistic ones among the committee members pointed to the fort's elegant 11 point star shape, and they also agreed that the statue should face southeast so that it would seem to be welcoming ships arriving from across the Atlantic.

A 1927 picture showing the 11 points of Fort Wood

With money in hand, the committee commissioned architect Richard Morris Hunt to design the pedestal, and by the end of 1881, he had his design submitted and approved. Hunt estimated he would have the nine story tall pedestal finished by the end of 1882. According to an article published in *Harper's Weekly*, "The pedestal designed by Mr. M. R. Hunt for Bartholdi's statue of "Liberty Enlightening the World," which is built inside the stone walls of the fort on Bedloe's Island, is worthy of the great figure that will stand on it. Architecturally it is, as it ought to be, not obtrusive in design or ornamentation, but its massiveness is sufficiently relieved by architectural variety and ornament to prevent an appearance of a mere pyramid of stone. The design is such that the pedestal calls no attention to itself, but directs it to the statue; and so modest is it in its appearance that a spectator would not be likely to guess how large and how high it is."

Hunt

Using his talent and training, Hunt brought together some of the best elements in American culture, marrying classical Doric portals with Aztec architectural features in ways that resembled the pyramid style of temple favored by ancient Americans. The *Harper's Weekly* article noted, "The foundation of the pedestal proper is 91 feet square at its base, and 66 feet 7 inches square at the top. It makes its pyramidal ascent, not with a continuous wall, but with a series of great layers of concrete, each one smaller than the one it rests on. The base of this foundation mass is 13 feet above the mean low-water mark, and its top 52 feet 10 inches. The pedestal, itself, therefore, begins at an elevation of 65 feet 10 inches, which is high above the stone walls of the fort. From these walls curved footways lead to the top of the foundation at the center of every side. Every side of the foundation and of the pedestal is alike. The solidity of this vast foundation work is broken only by wide passage- ways through it at a level with the ground, and a circular vertical shad in the middle, up which stairways and an elevator will run."

At that time, the elevator was still a new invention, but it would prove key to the construction and use of structures like the Statue of Liberty, as well as the many skyscrapers that would soon dot the New York City skyline. Still, the structure of the pedestal harkened more to the past than to the future. The *Harper's Weekly* article continued, "At its base the pedestal proper is 62 feet square. In the center of each side, at the base, is a doorway 5 feet wide and 13 feet high in the middle, to which the footways from the walls of the fort ascend. On either side of every door is a projecting disk of stone, on which will be placed the coats of arms of France and the United States in relief. A good architectural effect is produced by the rough-stone work at the corners of the pedestal. Above the doors there are on every side ten projecting stone disks, which, though they are 4 feet 6 inches in diameter, appear almost as small as mere beadwork to a spectator standing on the ground. On these the coats of arms of the States of the Union will be placed in relief."

While the article was accurate at the time in stating that the plan called for putting both French and American coats of arms on each disk, this carving never took place. By the time the money was raised to fund such an effort, the effect was no longer in style, so the disks remain bare to this day. Meanwhile, work on the pedestal was suspended until more funds could be raised.

An illustration depicting work on the pedestal

A picture of the pedestal under construction

Chapter 8: A Few Bits of Statistical Information

"To end this account, I ought to add to it a few bits of statistical information, although they have been published on various occasions. ... The statue is constructed of copper sheets, two and a half millimeters in thickness. It measures 46.08 meters [151 feet] from the base to the top of the torch, 35.50 meters [116.5 feet] from below the plinth to the crown.... The forefinger is 2.45 meters [8 feet] in length, and 1.44 meters [56.5 inches] in circumference at the second joint. The nail measures .35 meters [14 inches] by .26 meters [10 inches]. The head is 4.40 meters [14.5 feet] in height. The eye is .65 meters [25.5 inches] in width. The nose is I.I2 meters [44 inches] in length. About forty persons were accommodated in the head at the Universal Exposition of 1878. It is possible to ascend into the torch above the hand. It will easily hold twelve persons.

The total weight is about 200,000 kilos, of which 80,000 are copper and 120,000 iron. It represents an outlay of more than a million francs, including gifts, gratuitous work and the losses of all those who gave their devoted assistance to the work." - Frédéric Auguste Bartholdi

According to *Harper's Weekly*, "The ground was first broken for the erection of the pedestal in April, 1883; the excavation was begun in June; the laying of the foundation in October; and work was continued until December, 1884 — a period of eighteen months. Work was again begun on May 11, 1885, and the work will not be completed before it will have required nearly two years of continuous labor of as many men as can work on it The stone is from a quarry on Leete's Island in Connecticut, and the white-ness of the rough quoins gives a pleasant effect at a distance of several miles. These quoins are so heavy that the labor of lifting them to such a height has made the building of the pedestal one of the heaviest pieces of masonry ever done, even. In the vicinity of New York, where the piers of the East River Bridge stand as monuments of massive stone work. The total cost will not be less than $250,000. Colonel Charles P. Stone, the engineer-in-chief, has as large a force of men as can work on the structure at once, and it will be finished as rapidly as possible. The pedestal has been built to stand for all time to come."

Still worried about the possibility that another city might yet take the statue from New York City, Joseph Pulitzer offered to publish in his paper, the *New York World*, the name of anyone who gave any donation, great or small. Over the next several months, various notes appeared in its pages referencing those who donated to the cause. For example, the paper cited a " young girl alone in the world" who donated "60 cents, the result of self-denial," the donation of "five cents as a poor office boy's mite toward the Pedestal Fund," as well as a dollar sent by children from "the money we saved to go to the circus with." Even a group of men living in a home for alcoholics raised $15.

On August 11, 1885, the *New York World* joyfully exclaimed that more than $100,000 had been raised, with the vast majority of the donations coming from people giving a dollar or less. As the money continued to come in, work on the pedestal began again. Heading up the building project was retired General Charles Pomeroy Stone. He had begun supervising the men digging the 15 foot deep foundation for the project in 1883, and they finished the foundation in time for the cornerstone to be laid in 1884.

General Stone

While Hunt had hoped the pedestal could be made of solid granite, those funding the project suggested rather forcefully that he look for a less expensive option, so Lady Liberty has always stood on concrete walls that are faced with granite. That said, this base was impressive in its own right, as its 20 feet thick walls were the largest poured up until that time in history. The *Harper's* article noted in 1885, "This is the line that has now been reached in construction; above it the more elaborate superstructure begins. Above the disks are large panels 23 feet 6 inches long and 5 .feet 3 inches high, on which there will be appropriate inscriptions and designs. At an elevation of 72 feet 8 inches the walls of the pedestal are to recede, leaving on every side between them and two large columns and two pilasters a balcony on which doors from the inside open. This balcony is 5 feet 8 inches in width, and extends along the wall from comer pillar to comer pillar. The view from the balcony, on one side, of New York City, Brooklyn, Governor's Island, New Jersey, and the East River Bridge, and on the other, of Staten Island and the Bay — will be among the finest that can be enjoyed anywhere in the vicinity of New York. Above these pillars the pedestal becomes smaller, and its upper platform is 39 feet 4 inches square. By reason of the steps on the sides of the foundation, the doors in the lower part of the pedestal, the pediments, the projecting stone disks, the panels and the balcony, what would otherwise have been the monotonous walls of a pyramid, have been relieved so as to produce a good architectural effect, and at the same time to give the appearance of the great elevation to the statue itself, and not to the pedestal. On this surface, nearly forty feet square, the gigantic statue will stand, its footstool 89 feet above the mean low-water mark. The statue is 151 feet 1 inch high, and the top of the torch will be at an elevation of 305 feet 11 inches from mean low-water mark."

Of course, no matter what style it employed, the pedestal was merely meant to draw attention to the great statue that sits upon it. In fact, one author observed that the pedestal "craggily evokes the power of an ancient Europe over which rises the dominating figure of the Statue of Liberty." When he finally came to America in see his great statue put in place, Bartholdi insisted that another platform be built at its top from which Liberty herself rises.

On June 17, 1885, the steamer Isère arrived in New York Harbor from France bearing her precious cargo. More than 200,000 people stood along the docks or went out in boats to watch the ship arrive, but even at this point, the pedestal was not yet ready (and would not be until the spring of 1886). Nevertheless, the pieces of the statue began to be uncrated and taken to the island to be reassembled. Steel I-beams were first anchored into the concrete to hold the Lady's iron bones in place, and when this was completed, her beautiful copper skin was carefully attached. The size and shape of the statue made it impossible to use scaffolding, so the workers attached the copper into place while hanging from ropes.

A painting depicting the arrival of the statue in New York Harbor

When Bartholdi's plans to put floodlights on the torch's balcony to light it were nixed by the Army Corps of Engineers, he instead cut potholes into the gold leaf covered torch and lit it from within. The city built a special electrical power plant on the island to power the statue's electrical needs, and the famed architect Frederick Law Olmstead personally supervised the island's clean-up and landscaping.

Olmstead

On October 28, 1886, President Grover Cleveland, himself a native of New York, presided over the unveiling of the statue. That morning, one of the largest parades in the city's history wove its way through the streets with as many as 1 million people watching. When it finally made its way past the New York Stock Exchange, traders hanging out windows threw pieces of the ticker tape on to the passing marchers, making the event New York City's the first "ticker tape parade."

A painting depicting the unveiling of the Statue of Liberty

After the parade was over, Cleveland and the other dignitaries took a yacht across the port to Bedloe's Island for the statue's formal dedication. Many men spoke that day from both sides of the Atlantic, but it fell to the famous orator Chauncey M. Depew to give the final speech. He concluded his remarks by observing, "In all ages the achievements of man and his aspirations have been represented in symbols. Races have disappeared and no record remains of their rise or fall, but by their monuments we know their history…this Statue of Liberty rises toward the heavens to illustrate an idea which…inspired the charter in the cabin of the Mayflower and the Declaration of Independence from the Continental Congress…But, for unnumbered centuries to come, as Liberty levels up the people to higher standards and a broader life, this statue will grow in the admiration and affections of mankind…The rays from this beacon, lighting this gateway to the continent, will welcome the poor and the persecuted with the hope and promise of homes and citizenship. It will teach them that there is room and brotherhood for all who will support our institutions and aid in our development; but that those who come to disturb our peace and dethrone our laws are aliens and enemies forever. I devoutly believe that from the unseen and the unknown, two great souls have come to participate in this celebration. The faith in which they died fulfilled, the cause for which they battled triumphant, the people they loved in the full enjoyment of the rights for which they labored and fought and suffered, the spirit voices of Washington and Lafayette join in the glad acclaim of France and the United States to Liberty Enlightening the World."

Bibliography

Bell, James B.; Abrams, Richard L. (1984). *In Search of Liberty: The Story of the Statue of Liberty and Ellis Island.* Garden City, New York: Doubleday & Co.

Khan, Yasmin Sabina (2010). *Enlightening the World: The Creation of the Statue of Liberty.* Ithaca, New York: Cornell University Press.

Mitchell, Elizabeth (2014). *Liberty's Torch: The Great Adventure to Build the Statue of Liberty.* Grove/Atlantic, Inc. Kindle Edition.

Moreno, Barry (2000). *The Statue of Liberty Encyclopedia.* New York City: Simon & Schuster.

Sutherland, Cara A. (2003). *The Statue of Liberty.* New York City: Barnes & Noble Books.

Printed in Great Britain
by Amazon